WILDLIFE
of
SOUTH AFRICA

Text
David Steele

Photography
Photo Access, Cape Town:
CF Bartlett pp.97(t),102(b),104,148.
JJ Brooks pp.44,45(b),112,146,147.
Terry Carew pp.4,5,26(b),36(b),40,59(b),68,69,92(t),
94(b),95,98,101,113(t),129(t),138(b),141(b).
Koos Delport pp.21(b),85(t),124(b).
GPL du Plessis pp.11(b),19(t),30(t),36(t),46(t),47,50,
51(b),55,59(t),62,63,66(b),70,71(b),80,84,94(t),99,
106(t),136(t).
Lex Hes pp. 1,12(t),13-16,21(t),23,27,30(b),34,64,65(b),
67,76(b),77,81,85(b),86,88,89,91,93(b),100,107(b),
108(t),109(t,c,b),144,149.
FM Hodgson pp.54(b),58(t).
Val Johnstone p. 11(t).
Jean Laurie p.135(t).
Jean Morris pp.32(b),78.
W Ochojski pp.107(t),139(t).
Peter Pickford pp.10,12(b),17,33,35,38,39,42,43,48,49,52,
53,57,58(b),60,66,74,75,87,96,113(b),117(b),138(t),150-152.
Ernst Rohe p.56.
Jill Sneesby pp.22(b),32(t),102(t),124(t),128(t),134,
140(b).
David Steele pp.9,18,19(b),20,22(t),24-26(t),28,29,31,
37,41(t),46(b),51(t),61,72,73,76(t),79(t),103,110.111,
116,117(t),120,133(t).
Peter Steyn pp.41(b),45(t),71(t),97(b),105,106(b),
108(b),118,119,121-123,136(br),139(b),140(t),142,143,
145.
EL van Hooff pp.79(b),82,83.
Barrie Wilkins pp.90,92(b),93(t),114,115,125-127,128(b),129(b),
130-132,133(b),135(b),136(bl),137,141(t).

Design
Teddy Hartshorn

Commissioning
Trevor Hall
Andrew Preston

Editorial
Pauline Graham
Fleur Robertson
Gill Waugh

Production
Gerald Hughes
Ruth Arthur

Publishing Director
David Gibbon

CLB 2232
© 1989 Colour Library Books Ltd, Godalming, Surrey, England.
All rights reserved.
This edition published 1989 by Central News Agency Ltd,
Laub Street, New Centre, Johannesburg, South Africa.
Colour separations by Hong Kong Graphic Arts Ltd, Hong Kong.
Printed and bound in South Africa by CTP Printers.
ISBN 0 86283 698 0

WILDLIFE
of
SOUTH AFRICA

David Steele

Contents

Silhouetted against an orange sky, two giraffe browse on the leaves of an acacia in Kruger National Park. A korhaan greets the new day with its distinctive call, while a lioness and her cubs bask in the warmth of the first rays of a rising sun. Across the subcontinent, the early morning light paints the dunes of the Namib purple and gold whilst a gemsbok wanders across them. In the game reserves, visitors have been awake for an hour or more and are setting out in vehicles, or even on foot, to enjoy another day in the unspoilt wilderness areas of southern Africa.

Africa, in many ways, is still a dark continent. Poverty, war, plague, drought, disease and famine ravage its countries and its people. Southern Africa, though more prosperous than most of its northern neighbours, has not entirely escaped these horrors. And in some areas, in common with the rest of Africa, the territory is also facing the worst threat of all – the consequences of an uncontrolled population explosion.

What chance then does the wildlife of Africa, and particularly the wildlife of southern Africa, have as we approach the twenty-first century?

Not much, perhaps, judging by the fate of the black rhino. This magnificent creature, which is killed for its horn, is undoubtedly the most critically endangered large mammal in Africa today, and has been hunted to the point of extinction in most of the countries where it is found. During the 1970s and 1980s, poachers slaughtered over ninety-four per cent of the African population, and the brutal destruction is continuing.

In 1970, Africa had a population of 65 000 black rhino. By 1988, only 3 800 remained. During the same period, Kenya's black rhino population crashed from 18 000 to 500. In 1985, Zimbabwe lost over 100 rhino to poachers in the Zambesi Valley, and the war between government troops and poachers escalated. By 1988, the last five black rhino in Uganda had been wiped out. There was also talk of anti-government guerrillas in Angola funding their war effort with rhino horn and ivory, and of these items passing through Namibia on their way to international markets.

The only hope for the black rhino seems to lie in South Africa. Although there have been cases of poaching, including heavy poaching in the Kaokoveld of northern Namibia during the 1970s and early 1980s, which cut the black rhino population from 250 to fifty-five, the southern African population increased from 150 in 1930 to its present 600, largely as a result of the efforts of the Natal Parks Board. Having saved the white rhino from extinction, the Board conserved and built up the number of black rhino in Zululand. Today, the largest black rhino population in South Africa, about 220 animals, is found in the Hluhluwe/Umfolozi complex and the Board has also relocated over a hundred black rhino to other sanctuaries, more than fifty of which went to Kruger National Park. At the moment there are nine populations of the original South African black rhino, and one population each of the Namibian and East African subspecies, in South Africa.

Despite the limited success, there is no room for complacency, for if the rhino war on South Africa's borders is not contained, it will spill over into South Africa and there will be a bitter battle in the last stronghold of the black rhino. In fact, it may even have started with the rhinos recently poached in Swaziland and in eastern Transvaal.

In addition to the white rhino, the bontebok and Cape mountain zebra were both brought back from the brink of extinction during the second half of this century. But, to put things back into perspective, we must not forget that during the two centuries preceding this period, three species – the blue buck, the Cape lion and the quagga – were lost forever.

There are many dedicated people in southern Africa who are fighting to ensure that no more species are added to this list. Animals have found sanctuary in Kruger National Park and in Zululand's Hluhluwe, Umfolozi and St Lucia game reserves for nearly a hundred years. Many other reserves in southern Africa have been in existence for more than fifty years. The black states of southern Africa, too, are doing much to conserve their game.

As a result of the strenuous conservation efforts, southern Africa supports the widest variety of wildlife in Africa and offers the best opportunities for viewing it, which is why tourists are flocking to the subcontinent. But what is it that gives southern Africa such a wide variety of species to conserve and enjoy? The answer is simple: the wide variety of habitats that exist within the subcontinent. Southern Africa can loosely be divided into six major ecological regions:

NORTHERN REGION OF WOODLAND
Woodland has been described as "a growth of trees with crowns that do not touch." There are three main types of woodland: woodland proper, bushveld and savanna. Woodland proper has broad-leaved trees that are often deciduous and may cover enormous areas. Bushveld is

woodland with a dense and scrubby mixture of broad- and small-leaved trees and bushes which are often thorny. Open woodland, mainly acacia, with a ground cover of grass, is known as savanna. These three types of woodland may often be found in close proximity to one another.

Northern Zululand (Hluhluwe, Umfolozi, Mkuzi and Ndumu), the eastern Transvaal (Kruger National Park and the private game reserves), northern Transvaal, parts of Botswana (Chobe and Moremi) and northern Namibia (Etosha) fall within this northern woodland region. Further north, Mozambique, Zimbabwe, Zambia and Angola all have large areas of woodland. This is prime game country, and it is in these habitats that most of the larger and better-known species are found.

CENTRAL PLATEAU
This region includes two very important veld types – karoo and grassland. The Karoo is part of the large area of semi-desert which covers central southern Africa. It is largely an area of stony flats, broken by flat-topped hills and low mountains. The vegetation is scrubby, with little grass, and thorn trees and bushes grow along water courses. The Karoo is also noted for its variety of succulents. Important nature reserves established in the Karoo include Mountain Zebra National Park near Cradock, Karoo National Park near Beaufort West, and Karoo Nature Reserve near Graaff-Reinet.

Grassland, or grassveld, is found in the higher altitudes of the central plateau. The vegetation, as its name suggests, consists mainly of grasses and there are very few trees. The best areas of grassland are in the Transvaal Highveld and the Natal Midlands. These are now major agricultural areas and much of the wildlife, which consisted of species like blesbok, black wildebeest and springbok, has disappeared and there are no major game reserves to speak of.

SOUTHERN REGION
Situated in southern Cape Province, this is a region of winter rainfall. It is famous for its characteristic fynbos, which is also known as Cape flora or macchia.

Cape flora is one of the six floral kingdoms in the world, and its characteristic plants are proteas, ericas and reeds, interpersed with dainty gladioli, freesias, babanias, watsonias, nerinas and some interesting ground orchids, including the disas.

This is a fairly concentrated region, with far fewer reserves than it warrants, although the fynbos is protected in the many mountains of the area. The Cape of Good Hope Reserve, near Cape Town, which receives many visitors, and Bontebok National Park, near Swellendam, both lie within this region.

EASTERN REGION
This region receives summer rainfall and consists largely of grassland and evergreen forest. Some outstanding coastal forests occur along the Transkei and Zululand coasts. Mangroves may also grow along the estuaries and lagoons in these areas, from the Transkei northwards. Lake St Lucia, in particular, has some fine stands of mangrove.

The evergreen forests are generally situated in areas of high rainfall and mist belts, and they cover a very small proportion of southern Africa. The Knysna and Tsitsikama forests are the best and largest examples, although isolated pockets occur along the escarpment of Natal and the eastern Transvaal. Tsitsikama Forest National Park lies within the Tsitsikama Forest.

THE WESTERN REGION
The western region is southern Africa's desert region and is bordered by the Kalahari and the Karoo to the east, by bushveld to the north and fynbos to the south. The Namib desert, which covers the northern part of this region, is a true desert, with some of the largest and most widely spread dunes in the world. Years may pass without any rainfall and the animals obtain the moisture they require from the mists which roll in from the cold Atlantic Ocean.

South of the Namib, across the Orange River, lies Namaqualand. After winter rains, the arid plains of Namaqualand briefly come alive in in a blaze of colour as flowers carpet the veld and produce one of the most scenic wonders of southern Africa.

THE COASTLINE
Southern Africa has an interesting and varied coastline. Although much of the western coastline has dunes and arid plains stretching down to the cold waters, it is also one of the richest fishing grounds in the world. Here, seals and pelagic (fish-eating) birds compete with man to harvest the waters. The coast is dotted with many small islands, and some of these have been made into reserves. Bird Island, at Lamberts Bay, which is linked to the mainland by causeway, is the most accessible.

Further south, near Cape Town, is Langebaan Lagoon and National Park, which is of international importance because of the tens of thousands of waders it supports.

The warm Mozambique current gives the east coast its mild climate and rich vegetation. Tsitsikama Coastal National Park, north of Plettenberg Bay, conserves a pristine stretch of coastline, and there are marine reserves further north, on the Zululand coast, which protect valuable turtle nesting grounds.

The game areas of southern Africa are extremely accessible. Of the reserves and national parks featured in this book, all of them, with the exception of Moremi in Botswana, can be visited in normal passenger vehicles, and they are all included in tour itineraries offered by various operators. There are regular flights into Kruger National Park, which has an airport near Skukuza, Etosha and Botswana, and the larger private reserves also have their own landing strips.

The best time to visit these wildlife sanctuaries, from a game-viewing point of view, is during the dry winter months. At this time large herds congregate around certain waterholes, where they may attract predators. A different atmosphere prevails in summer, when fresh green scenery, thunderstorms, wild flowers and newborn animals are the main attraction.

At the time of writing, all the reserves mentioned in this book had escaped the strife that has occurred in certain parts of southern Africa, and could be regarded as 'safe' destinations. The main danger is from mosquitos, and anti-malaria tablets are necessary in all the reserves except those in the extreme south.

The rest camps throughout southern Africa are generally clean, comfortable and well-equipped. In addition to the various types of accommodation they offer, most of them, with the exception of those in Botswana and Zululand, have shops and restaurants. Many of the reserves also operate guided wilderness trails from which participants are able to explore the wilderness areas on foot. In recent years these trails have become very popular and, as is the case with accommodation, may have to booked a year in advance.

After reading this book, some people might like to try their hand at wildlife photography. We will assume that they are well-versed in the basics of photography, but need some extra tips prior to photographing in a game reserve.

Which is the best reserve, photographically speaking? This is a difficult question, and you should not only consider the variety and abundance of game in a reserve, but the vegetation as well. No matter how prolific and interesting the game of a reserve is, it is of little use to the photographer if it is continually hidden behind trees. Etosha, for example, is as perfect for photography as any of the other reserves, boasting numerous waterholes that present exciting opportunities, but it does lack some of the advantages of the other reserves in that it has no hides.

Some reserves have hides which are marvellous for photography. Mkuzi, Umfolozi and Hluhluwe have superb hides for winter (dry-season) photography. Other reserves have wilderness trails, which should interest most photographers. There are several in Kruger National Park, and most of South Africa's other national parks have a wilderness trail, as do Zululand's Umfolozi and Lake St Lucia. Others, like Mkuzi and Ndumu, have interesting walks where you can go into the bush for half a day, accompanied by a game guard.

If money is not a problem, the best reserves to visit for photographic purposes are the private ones, especially those in the eastern Transvaal, as well as those in Zululand and Botswana.

With regard to still photography, transparency or slide films are generally the most rewarding and are essential if you ever hope to sell reproduction rights on your work. If you want large colour prints, then colour negative film is probably the best choice.

The most useful camera is the 35mm single lens reflex with through-the-lens metering. The 35mm format is preferred because of the wide range and low price of the lenses as compared with similar quality lenses for medium format cameras. A good telephoto lens is essential for detailed wildlife photography. A combination of lenses is even better. Besides a standard lens, a very good combination would be a 200mm, 400mm and 600mm lens. This may seem extravagant, but the 200mm is not powerful enough for some work, while the 600mm would be too powerful for most shots.

When travelling through a reserve it is best to have a 200mm or 300mm lens attached to your camera. When you suddenly come upon an animal you want to photograph, you can take your initial shots quickly with this easy-to-use combination. Having achieved this, and if the game has not been frightened away, a longer lens may be attached for still greater magnification. It is at times like this that fellow passengers can become useful assistants.

With the bright light found in southern Africa, a film with a rating of 50 to 100 ASA is recommended. This is fast enough for the early morning or late afternoon shots and for moving animals, yet it is slow enough to get your background out of focus when photographing a close-up. Whether 'shooting' game, birds, insects or flowers, most close-ups will be enhanced by having the background out of focus, as this might otherwise detract from the main subject.

When using a lens more powerful than 300mm, some support is necessary for the camera and lens. The cheapest and most convenient is a bean bag on the car window, although some photographers may prefer a sturdy tripod head which can be clamped to a car window. When photographing, a golden rule is to switch the car engine off to avoid unnecessary vibrations.

Most of the above refers to video filming as well as to still work. Camera steadiness is very important when filming on video, as any movement will be obvious on the screen. When filming in a game reserve, it is important to have continuity shots to link the animal scenes together. Ideas for such shots include people viewing or photographing game from inside their cars, scenes taken at the rest camps and, need you be reminded, the inevitable sunset.

As well as giving you a vivid record of your visit to the game reserve, the beauty of wildlife photography is that it enables you to share some of the wonders of nature with others. In addition, advanced photographers will find that most national and international salons have categories in which they can enter their wildlife shots in competition with others.

Facing page: a giraffe browses on the choicest leaves of a Bushveld tree at dawn.

Bushveld Country

The Bushveld, or Lowveld, is situated in the eastern Transvaal, between the Escarpment and Mozambique and between Zimbabwe and Swaziland. Rich in folklore, its recent history is well documented and it is famous as the home of South Africa's favourite treasure – the Kruger National Park.

Some outstanding game reserves are situated adjacent to the Kruger National Park, including Mala Mala, possibly the world's most famous private game reserve, Londolozi, Sabi Sabi and Timbavati. In these exclusive reserves visitors tour in Land-Rovers which leave the roads to approach game, and game viewing is also permitted at night.

The park's two potentially hostile international borders give cause for concern and there is currently a problem with refugees entering the park from war-ravaged Mozambique.

Facing page: an aerial view of typical Bushveld country, complete with a herd of elephants. Top: storm clouds gather over the Bushveld, and (above) bush gives way to woodland and a cluster of hauntingly beautiful fever trees.

Above: two zebra stallions square up to each other, frightening a group of young impala (left), while a kudu cow and her attendant red-billed oxpecker (facing page) remain ever alert. Overleaf: a group of giraffes keeping a careful watch in all directions.

Above: an elephant relaxing at a Bushveld waterhole, (left) a lone elephant in the mist and (facing page) a pair of elephants about to enjoy a river drink.

A fabulous variety of birds thrive in the Bushveld, including the red-crested korhaan (facing page), seen here calling early in the morning, (right) the European roller, a colourful summer migrant to the area, and (below) the ground hornbill, which normally walks through the Bushveld in groups.

Kruger National Park

The Kruger is South Africa's largest national park, covering about two per cent of the country's total land area. The special attraction of the park is its great variety and large numbers of game. However, with few exceptions, the terrain does not allow for views of large herds of animals, and there is always an element of anticipation along the winding tourist roads. The bird life of the park is rich and varied, including some 450 different species.

In spite of its many visitors, the park is so large and so well organised that each visit, no matter how brief, remains a precious individual experience. There are a number of rest camps offering facilities from camping to comfortable, air-conditioned bungalows.

Left: elephants and giraffes pass each other on the banks of the Olifants River. Kruger National Park is a haven for butterflies, including the common African monarch (above). Below: a pair of Burchell's zebra greet each other.

By far the greatest attraction for the average visitor to the park are the three types of large cat: lion, leopard and cheetah. Left: a lioness on the prowl, (below) a leopard resting beside a termite mound and (facing page) a cheetah on the lookout for game. Overleaf: African buffalo, of which there are so many in the park that culling is necessary.

Above left: a solitary sable antelope and young, more usually found in a nursery herd formed by females for the protection of their young. Left: warthogs are found widely in the northern parts of South Africa. Litters of up to five young are born at a time, but mortality is high. Above: young impala group together in nursery herds with adult females and a territorial male. They are particularly common in Kruger National Park, where most births occur in late November. Right: a lioness rests in the late afternoon sun at the edge of a pan, accompanied by her cubs.

Cheetah cubs (above) spend about eighteen months with their mother. They have a light-coloured mantle when born, presumably aiding camouflage when their mother has to leave them hidden in grass. A leopard cub (facing page) has long, woolly fur and will become independent at about fourteen months.

Sophisticated electronic equipment, patience and skill provide scenes of birds feeding their young that no human eye could ever see unaided. Left: a brown-hooded kingfisher, complete with prey, approaches its burrow, and (below) a pearl-breasted swallow is greeted by its chicks. Facing page: (top) a hoopoe feeding its chick, and (bottom) a male paradise flycatcher bringing a dragonfly to its nest.

A number of birds may be seen at waterholes. One of the most beautifully coloured is the small malachite kingfisher (facing page). Not quite as eye-catching is the handsome blue crane (right), the national bird of South Africa. A darter (below) will often perch, with wings spread out to dry, on rocks or a branch close to water.

Zululand

Zululand's game reserves have a special character. Some animals which are rarely seen elsewhere in southern Africa are fairly common in Zululand. These include white rhino, nyala, hippo, crocodile and warthog. The scenery and vegetation has its own character, too.

The most important reserves, from south to north, are the Lake St Lucia complex, Umfolozi, Hluhluwe, Mkuzi and Ndumu.

Lake St Lucia is primarily a reserve for hippos, crocodiles, aquatic birds and, of course, the fragile lake itself. The twin reserves of Umfolozi and Hluhuwe, connected by a 'corridor', are famous as the home of the white rhino. Once gravely endangered, this species is now in much less danger of extinction than the black rhino, which is also found in the area.

Mkuzi is something of a Mecca for wildlife photographers. The hides and pans provide frequent opportunities for photography. Ndumu, which is situated on the Mozambique border, is more tropical and ranks as the top birding spot in Zululand, if not in South Africa.

Zululand is a great sanctuary for crocodiles (left) – this specimen was photographed at Ndumu. Warthogs (bottom left) are common in Zululand and are frequently seen at Mkuzi, while waterbuck (below) are always found close to water. Bottom: nyala drink at the edge of a Ndumu pan against a backdrop of fever trees. The gregarious blue wildebeest (overleaf) is found in the main reserves of Zululand.

Rhino (these pages) are severely endangered in Africa. It was in Hluhluwe and Umfolozi in Zululand that the white rhino was saved from extinction. As may be seen from these photos, it has since thrived, and attention is now being focussed on the desperate plight of the black rhino.

Mkuzi Game Reserve in Zululand has a magnificent network of game viewing hides – this group of giraffes (facing page) was photographed as it cautiously approached one of them. Buffalo (below) and white rhino (bottom) may also be observed from hides in Zululand's reserves.